HELP!

My Child Isn't Reading Yet –

What Should I Do?

How to Get the Right Help for Your Struggling or Dyslexic Reader.

By Susan Crawford

No part of this book may be reproduced or transmitted in any form or by any means, electronic or mechanical, including photocopying, recording, or by any information storage and retrieval system, without permission in writing from the author.

Copyright © 2013
By Susan Crawford
New York, NY
All Rights Reserved

ISBN-10: 148012334X
ISBN-13: 9781480123342

Dedication

To everyone who has helped

me along this journey

Table of Contents

Introduction

Chapter 1:   Take Care of Yourself 1

Chapter 2:   Does Anything Here Sound Familiar? 3

Chapter 3:   You're Not Alone 9

Chapter 4:   What Causes Reading Problems? 11

Chapter 5:   How Are Reading Problems Helped? 23

Chapter 6:   Help! What to Do First, What to Do Next 35

Chapter 7:   Who's In Charge Here? 39

Chapter 8:   ABC's of IDEA 47

Chapter 9:   Your Action Plan 63

Chapter 10: Your Plan In Action 71

Chapter 11: Your Struggling Reader At Home 99

Chapter 12: Closing Thoughts 111

Resources 115

References 119

INTRODUCTION

I've written this book to share with you information that I've shared with many parents one-on-one or in small groups for more than a decade. It is based on my own experiences "navigating the system," as parents say, and finding the right kind of help when my own two then-struggling readers needed it. We live in New York City, so my experiences reflect navigation of that particular system. Different states have different levels of awareness of reading difficulties, and their school districts reflect those differences. Some states are much more involved in helping struggling readers within their schools, others much less so. (Part of your "navigation" will be to find out where your state and school district fit into this picture.)

My goal is to give you a framework for what you can do to help your struggling reader, what you should be able to expect in terms of help, and what you will need to do to get that help. I am not a lawyer or clinician or an academically-trained reading expert, but I am a parent who has been where you are. From my experiences, I can provide you with a "ladder" of actions that will lead you to help that could otherwise take you a long time to figure out on your own. That is, in fact, why I have written this book. Every parent I have ever tried to help seemed to be discovering for him- or herself what needed to be done as if for the first time. They had no roadmap to follow, no guideposts to let them know what to look for and to expect at each intersection, and no way to evaluate whether what was being done to help their struggling readers would really work. It was as if each parent had to figure out how to proceed from scratch. This book is what I would have liked to have had when I started out on that journey!

As more and more parents learn to advocate for help for their struggling readers, my hope is that it will prompt school districts to be more responsive, and to provide the help to these students that districts are legally supposed to be providing.

My hope is also that this book will bring you "up to speed" quickly on what to ask for, how to ask for it, and how to get help quickly. The sooner your struggling child gets the right help, the sooner he or she – and you - will no longer be struggling!

(A note about "notes" – in the e-book version of this book I provided hyperlinks to source material throughout the book. For the print version, links noted with numbers throughout the book are listed together by chapter in the back under "References.")

CHAPTER 1

TAKE CARE OF YOURSELF

When I first outlined this book, this was going to be the last chapter. After all, the focus of the book is your struggling reader and what you can do to help him or her (or them!). With the advantage of hindsight, though, I can say that it is crucial you know that this is not an issue you are going to resolve in a matter of weeks or even months. From the time you might first have an inkling your child is having trouble reading, to the time he or she has gotten appropriate help and has the proper supports in place in school, it could easily take two years. And that's if you're staying on top of the situation! Many parents don't learn their children have reading problems until well into elementary school or even later. They and their children struggle through a period that can last years.

If you are prepared for a time-frame of at least two years, then you should actually be able to calm down and make sure you are taking care of yourself, as well as your struggling reader, throughout this process. That means making sure you eat properly, get enough sleep and exercise, and otherwise not lose yourself in a "world of worry." Don't let attention to your health get relegated to "when I have time," or "when this gets settled." Imagine my alarm when I found out, five years into getting my first son "settled," that my second son was now going to need the same help! (At least by then I knew exactly what to do.) So make sure to keep yourself on your agenda. Your children need calm and healthy adults around them throughout this process.

CHAPTER 2

DOES ANYTHING HERE SOUND FAMILIAR?

Your child adored playing in pre-school, but dreads going to "big boy/girl" school.

Other kids seem to be picking up reading while your first grader prefers to draw or play.

Other kids seem to zip through their homework. Your second grader prefers to draw or play.

At home your child loves to play with friends and siblings, but getting her to focus on homework is a nightly battle.

He occupies himself for hours with blocks or Lego, but won't let you leave his side while he does homework.

She talks a blue streak but can't stand to read or write.

Handwriting is hard to read and spelling is either wildly "inventive" or overly-phonetic.

His teacher says that at school he is often staring off into space, or drawing.

You think she is reading aloud "early reading" books she has brought home from school. After a few weeks or months you discover she is actually reciting these books, having heard her teacher read them in school.

You discover the teacher has placed him next to a super-organized child to help him find the right page to read, or the right math problem, and to otherwise keep him "on task."

You think your first grader just spent a half hour on homework, but when you go into his room to check up, you discover he's been drawing a picture. Great picture, but now "homework time" has to start all over!

Your second grader is great at math, but reading still isn't happening.

You are told your son is not "focusing" and the school wants you to have him tested for ADD/ADHD.

At a parent-teacher conference you are told your son is the "class clown," and that he does not appear to be reading yet.

At a parent-teacher conference you are told your daughter always needs to go to the bathroom at "read-aloud" time.

Your fourth-grader still wants you to sit by her side through nightly homework -- no matter how long it takes.

Your fifth-grader zips through his homework willy-nilly, but is completely focused and diligent about practicing his guitar.

Your sixth grader is gregarious and has lots of friends, many of whom help him with his homework.

Your seventh-grader breezes through math, but gets points off for "not showing her work," because she does much of it in her head.

In group projects your eighth-grader always offers to do the artwork.

Your ninth-grader plays piano beautifully but can't read a note of music. Instead he picks it up by ear or by watching his teacher's hands.

You suddenly move your tenth grader to a private school where graduation will not depend on high-stakes "exit" exams.

All the way up through the grades, from kindergarten through high school, "undiscovered" struggling readers are found. Some even thrive. That gregarious sixth-grader whose friends help with homework? He has already learned, whether he knows it or not, to delegate tasks that are a struggle for him. In fact, while a fifth of the general population is dyslexic, fully one-third of small business owners in the U.S. are dyslexic[1]. They are able to carve out a niche in what they do well, such as sales, design, or marketing, tasks that do not call for a lot of reading and writing, then delegate the rest. *Fortune* magazine even ran an article on "Dyslexic CEOs."[2] Some do not know they are dyslexic until they are adults,[3] if ever, or until their children are diagnosed with it. Even wild success, though, cannot always erase the pain and isolation these struggling readers felt back in school.

Indeed, some who cannot overcome their reading struggles are overtaken by them instead. It is an American tragedy that upwards of 70% of the population in many U.S. prisons either cannot read, or struggle with it.

CHAPTER THREE

YOU'RE NOT ALONE

While the scenarios in the preceding chapter might be all too familiar to you, when you go to your child's parent/teacher conferences you might be left with the impression that he or she is the only one in the class with these struggles. Don't believe it! In fact, four out of ten children in the U.S. struggle with learning to read. That's according to the National Institute of Child Health and Human Development (NICHD). Of those children, fully half, or 20%, are dyslexic. Boys and girls are affected equally, although there is a prevailing assumption that more boys than girls are dyslexic. That is only because it is more likely to cause boys to act out, while dyslexic girls are more likely to withdraw.

People are always astonished when I tell them how prevalent reading difficulties are. The fact that these statistics are not better known speaks to why the help your child needs is not, in most places, automatically offered. Instead, it often has to be pried from school districts, sometimes even through lawsuits. That is in great measure because the law that established help for learning disabilities in 1975 -- now known as the Individuals with Disabilities Education Act (IDEA) -- has never been fully funded.

CHAPTER FOUR

WHAT CAUSES READING PROBLEMS?

How Big is the Problem?

In the 1990's The National Institute of Child Health and Human Development (NICHD) convened a Reading Panel to study why so many children fall through the cracks in their reading ability.

The Panel produced its report[4] in 2000, with the finding that four out of ten children still struggle with reading by fourth grade. That 40% then divides between the 20% of the population who are dyslexic, and 20% who struggle with learning to read for other reasons. Together, that adds up to nearly half our population of students! How can that be? Is it something in the water?

Who Is Affected By It?

As universal schooling took hold over the past two centuries, there came a point when it was clear that a certain proportion of students could not learn to read with the facility and ease of their fellow classmates. Some had difficulty learning to read, but finally did. Others left school in despair of ever learning to read at all. Incredibly, with all we now know about reading difficulties, that still happens! Indeed, the nation's high drop-out rate can easily be traced in great measure to struggling readers who are not helped.

The following passage describes the first recorded references to dyslexia:

> This condition was first recognized in 1896. It was first referred to by Kerr in the Howard Prize Essay of the Royal Statistical Society. Kerr discussed the needs of school children

and mentioned that there were children in the schools who had no physical defects and were well endowed as to general mental ability who could not learn to read and were not understood by their instructors. He recommended that they be taught in separate classes.

Morgan, an ophthalmologist, in 1896 reported the case of a boy of fourteen who was brought to him for examination of vision. The boy's parents thought that his inability to learn to read might be due to defect of vision. The vision was found to be perfect, the mentality of the boy to be good, but he confessed that "printed words had no meaning to him." Morgan applied the term "congenital word-blindness" to such cases." (Clara Schmitt, The Elementary School Journal, 1918.)[5]

There, in two short paragraphs, is a concise description of dyslexia, including a proposed solution -- "that they be taught in separate classes." Yet in the more than 100 years since these findings were recorded, incredibly little has been done to systematically help the nation's struggling readers and dyslexics who are not able to learn using standard classroom practices.

To get an idea of the practices in use at that time, one can see in a few other short paragraphs how Laura Ingalls Wilder learned to read *on the first day of school* in the book from her "Little House" series, *On the Banks of Plum Creek:*

> "Mary [Laura's older sister] showed Teacher how much she could read and spell. But Laura looked at Ma's book and shook her head. She could not read. She was not even sure of all the letters."
>
> "'Well, you can begin at the beginning, Laura,' said Teacher, 'and Mary can study further on.'"
>
> [A page later]
>
> "Laura was a whole class by herself [in the one-room schoolhouse], because she was the only pupil who could not read. Whenever Teacher had time, she called Laura to her desk and helped her read letters. Just before dinner-[lunch] time that first day, Laura was able to read C A T, cat. Suddenly she remembered and said 'P A T, Pat!'" [Laura was remembering seeing those letters on the side of her family's new stove, abbreviating "patent."]
>
> "Teacher was surprised. 'R A T, rat!' said Teacher. 'M A T, mat!' And Laura was reading! She could read the whole first row in the speller."[6]

By lunch-time!

Of course, it was Mary's first day of school too, so if she was already reading, it was from being home-schooled by "Ma." Presumably, Laura would have picked up something from hearing those lessons at home. We can also assume that Laura was not dyslexic!

The way both girls learned to read was not much different from the way I learned to read in the late 1950's/early 60's. By that time, study of letter sounds, or phonics, was combined with the "Look/Say" approach of Dick, Jane and Sally books. I remember building the same "word families" that Laura remembered for the "_at" family. I also remember loving to play hangman, "Phlounder," Scrabble, and "Ghost," or seeing how many other words I could find within a word like "contentment," or build from the letters of "establishment."

I loved words. My parents and siblings loved words. I grew up to be a writer. Then I had two children for whom the written word was an "enemy," a foreign interloper in their childhood world of play and exploration. Had I never read to them? Hardly! Did I park them in front of the TV? No. Did I speak in mono-syllabic sentences every other hour? Not at all. We lived in a word-fest of chatter, songs, books, and stories. Starting school seemed like it would just be the next stop on their way to the literate, literary, and literature-laden world in which I had grown up.

Not so fast!

Black lines against white paper were, for me, logical representations of the many words I had been surrounded by in the years before I started first grade. For my children, they were strange symbols with little or no connection to the spoken chatter they had heard, and to which they had contributed so much, in their pre-school years.

Reading is not "Natural"

The chief difference between written and spoken words for humans is that speaking is a natural, innate feature of our human development. Reading, on the other hand, is an acquired skill. In that sense, it is more like learning to play a musical instrument than like learning to speak.

We know from stories such as "The Wild Child,"[7] that children brought up in surroundings with no human, verbal stimulation will be hard-pressed to learn to speak. But those who are brought up in normal human surroundings pick up spoken language naturally, without the need to be taught. Even grammar is acquired naturally in settings where a child is learning a native tongue with native speakers.

Written words, on the other hand, are comprised of symbols that represent sounds. Learning to read for around 60% of children is, if not seamless, a natural outgrowth of speaking, singing, and drawing that they have done in their pre-school years. For that other 40%, it takes more than a leap of faith that those dark symbols against white paper represent sounds. It takes explicit, patient instruction. For half of those children – the dyslexics – it takes routes even more circuitous than direct instruction of phonics for them to translate those symbols to sounds, and then to store what those symbols represent in their memories.

Are these "reading problems?" "Reading disabilities?" Or are they simply "reading differences?" Whatever we choose to call them, they need more time and attention than is given in standard, early-grade reading instruction of the early 21st century.

There's a reason for that.

Whole Language Versus Phonics

Around 1970 reading instruction took a sharp turn from the phonetic approach used since Laura Ingalls Wilder's days, and even from the 20th century "Look/Say" contribution. It was called "Whole Language," and it assumed that children could learn to read just from hearing and seeing words.

Either way, as you can see by the NICHD statistics, relying on a "sight word" recognition approach would leave out a substantial portion of the population, for whom more direct and explicit instruction in word sounds and symbols is needed.

There are a multitude of reasons why whole language has taken root so strongly, and persisted for so long, despite equally persistent evidence that it is inadequate for a significant number of students. To explore all of those reasons is beyond the scope of this book, but it is certainly a subject for study by many in the literacy and education communities.

Why Don't All Children Learn to Read the Same Way?

Of the 40% of struggling readers, about half need more help with decoding skills. These are the skills that focus on phonics, or the sounds of letters and letter combinations, and phonemes, or the sounds within words, and the words into which these components build. Once these struggling readers have "cracked" that code, they can usually go on to be fluent readers without much more additional help.

Dyslexia, on the other hand, is caused by neural differences in the brain. These children do not have access to the same neural reading connections that their easier-reading peers have. This is the cause of the "word blindness" described in 1896. In more recent years, its physiological basis has been proven in fMRIs (functional magnetic resonance images), first in studies by Drs. Sally and Bennett Shaywitz at Yale University. (Drawings and photographs of these brain scans can be seen in Dr. Sally Shaywitz's book *Overcoming Dyslexia*,[8] as well as online.[9])

Not only do these neural differences make it harder for these children to read, but there is a genetic component as well. This aspect is being studied by another Yale research team[10] under Dr. Jeffrey Gruen, helping to explain why dyslexia often runs in families.

As it turned out, several members of my husband's family had had problems learning to read. Interestingly, these "learning differences" seem to have been taken more in stride in the 1950's and 1960's, when the "baby boom" generation was in school, than they are now. It was as if "the system" back then accepted that there was a certain proportion of the population who struggled with reading, even if the system didn't completely know what to do about it.

A central difference between then and now is that, despite how much more we know about reading difficulties, some components of "the system" have determined that failure is the best medicine for these students – through grade retention policies -- or for their schools – through closures.

Thus, even while the No Child Left Behind Act (NCLB) was passed by Congress in 2002 with one of its mandates being to identify struggling students in each school, little was done to adequately provide the sort of help those students, or their schools, need. The kind of help that should be provided was clearly described in the very Reading Panel Report of 2000 upon which NCLB was built!

CHAPTER FIVE

HOW ARE READING PROBLEMS HELPED?

The National Reading Panel Report of 2000 gives a clear explanation of what sorts of instruction are needed when students are learning to read. "The Panel found that for children to be good readers, they must be taught:

- phonemic awareness skills – the ability to manipulate the sounds that make up spoken language;

- phonics skills – the understanding that there are relationships between letters and sounds;

- the ability to read fluently with accuracy, speed, and expression; and

- to apply reading comprehension strategies to enhance understanding and enjoyment of what they read."[11]

Regarding struggling readers with learning disabilities, or who are low achievers,

"...systematic phonics instruction, combined with synthetic phonics instruction produced the greatest gains. Synthetic phonics instruction consists of teaching students to explicitly convert letters into phonemes and then blend the phonemes to form words." (For more on the Reading Panel's Report of 2000, visit the National Reading Panel's website.[12])

Recommendations of the Reading Panel were incorporated into the No Child Left Behind legislation primarily through its "Reading First" initiative. This provided a funding stream for early reading programs to low-income schools that would help bolster children's grasp of phonetics (sounds of letters and letter combinations) and phonemic awareness (discriminating among the sounds within words). A number of these programs proved beneficial in boosting reading scores in schools where they were used. However, the program fell victim to vendor scandals[13] by the mid 2000's, which ultimately sidelined the whole "Reading First" effort.

Another outgrowth of the Reading Panel's recommendations in its 2000 report was the Response to Intervention (RTI) protocol developed by the National Institute of Child Health and Human Development (NICHD) and introduced in 2004. The goal of RTI was to replace the "waiting to fail" model that had marked referral to Special Education and its special services. In that model, students had to be at least two years behind grade level in reading before they could be referred for Special Education services. However, RTI has been so slow to take root, that the "waiting to fail" model is effectively still the norm in many states.

The Reading Panel Report and RTI have given strong academic, clinical and moral support for specialized interventions to help struggling readers and dyslexics. Many different programs are now available, addressing different aspects of reading difficulties. These programs build upon the kinesthetic, multi-sensory program first developed by Samuel Orton and Anna Gillingham in the 1930's.

While "word blindness" had been described in 1896, it was Samuel Orton who codified dimensions of reading disabilities starting in the 1920's. The description in a scholarly paper that the National Center on Learning Disabilities provides on its website of Orton's work is extremely instructive in several respects. One is, of course, in describing the history of Orton's work. In another, we see how he was facing a similar "look-say"/"whole language" approach to reading in the 1920's that resurfaced in the 1950's, to be replaced by the even less explicit-instruction of "whole language" in the 1970's, and which still guides much of reading instruction in our schools today. No wonder so many struggling readers keep falling through the cracks!

According to Hallahan and Mercer, authors of the paper[14] on the NRCLD site, Orton "...was one of the first to advocate focusing on phonics instruction with students with reading disabilities. He criticized the then-current "look and say" or "sight reading" method of reading instruction for the general population..."

Orton also advocated for systematic teaching of sound blends within words, which we now call "phonemes." His findings informed the work of Anna Gillingham and Bessie Stillman in the 1930's which --"...emphasized building the following linkages: visual-auditory, auditory-visual, auditory-kinesthetic, and kinesthetic-visual. Gillingham and Stillman believed 'it is essential to establish each linkage with patient care, even into the thousandth repetition' (Gillingham & Stillman, 1936, p. 36)."[15]

That is a lot of repetition! But it helped, and the "Orton-Gillingham Approach" still forms the basis for intervention programs for struggling and dyslexic readers today.

Check out the NRCLD site for Hallahan and Mercer's full description of Orton's very important and seminal work, plus the American Education website.[16] The paper cited on the NRCLD site also gives a detailed account of the work of Orton's research assistant, Marion Monroe, and of Grace Fernald, who focused on the value of kinesthetic learning for struggling readers even before Orton did. Fernald also embraced more of a whole-language, or at least whole-word approach to teaching struggling readers, which likely led to her work being less well-known in reading intervention circles today.

In a rather extraordinary example of how prescient Samuel Orton's work was, the NRCLD paper describes Orton's theories about the role of brain hemispheric "dominance" in reading abilities and disabilities, and how they had been largely discounted. In a fascinating example of how fMRIs have brought our understanding of reading into sharp focus, however, a study[17] at Georgetown University in 2003 showed evidence to support those very theories of Orton's from many decades earlier.

Returning to current-day practices, for a reading intervention program to be effective, specialists need to be able to diagnose what is causing a child's reading problems, and to know which programs address those problems in particular. There is no one-size-fits-all program-in-a-box, or in-a-computer program, that can address the full range of reading problems.

The International Dyslexia Association has compiled a list of 50 programs that it considers appropriate as the sorts of "reading interventions" that struggling readers, and dyslexics in particular, need. They can be found in the IDA's "Matrix of Multisensory Structured Language Programs."[18]

How Do Reading "Interventions" Work?

Programs on the IDA matrix share two important features that distinguish them from classroom reading instruction. The first is that they are built around multi-sensory stimuli that involve forms of touch to complement stimulation of eyes and ears in learning to read. The second feature is that these programs are provided at a more intensive level than regular classroom reading and practice. This intensity can range from an extra period of work several times a week in small groups, such as in the Wilson Program, to school-wide programs such as Success for All. Full-time programs, such as Lindamood/Bell Learning Processes, works with students one-on-one for at least four hours a day, five days a week for, on average, six to twelve weeks (or more), depending on the severity of the disability.

As you can see, just these three programs offer differing levels of intensity, instruction and interaction. As a result, costs of interventions rise as a program becomes more individualized and more intensive. Success for All, for instance, includes a one-on-one component for the students who need it in a participating school that uses it. If we use the 20% figure for dyslexics in the general population, it is likely that in such a participating school, 20% of the students, at the very least,* may need some amount of one-on-one work for the program to succeed. However, that level of personal, one-on-one interaction is often the first to be dropped when schools have to cut costs. The Wilson Program has become popular in part because it is much more affordable for schools. The way it is set up, though, does not allow for the one-on-one, daily, intensive interaction that is the hallmark of the highest levels of interventions in the other two programs.

Lindamood/Bell (in the interest of full disclosure, this was one of the programs that we used for our family) provides full-time, one-on-one, high-intensity interventions of the kind recommended by the Reading Panel for dyslexics.

---

*I say "at least" because in many schools with high concentrations of struggling students, the proportions of struggling readers can be considerably higher than in the general population. That is because, in a given school district, there may be guidelines, such as a particular state's rules for federal Title 1 funding, which prompts districts to concentrate high-needs children in particular schools so the schools can receive that funding.)

However, in cases where these programs are not paid for by a school district, costs for that level of treatment are prohibitive for most families without having to borrow money.

How Should These Interventions Be Implemented?

There may be someplace in the country where a full array of appropriate interventions in line with the ideals of Response to Intervention, No Child Left Behind, and the Reading Panel are in place. I personally don't know of any, but if you do, please share it on the Right to Read Project blog![19]

In the meantime, it is likely you will need to patch together the services your child needs from among those the school or district provides on-site, and/or those your "team" advises, but that may only be available off-site.

To implement truly effective reading intervention programs, schools and districts may need to reconsider the overall pacing of their early school years. The ideal is for all children to be "on schedule" in their skills development for the type of instruction that builds upon itself from third and fourth grade onward. But that should not be at the expense of their childhoods! While the trend in the U.S. is to push academics into kindergarten and even pre-school, it is helpful to consider that in Finland, which has the highest overall test scores in the world, children are not even taught to read until they are 7! (Perhaps Laura Ingalls Wilder was able to pick up reading so quickly because she was already 8 when she started school?) Even so, Finnish students are tested for dyslexia when they arrive at school at age 5. So clearly, something is going on in Finnish classrooms in the intervening two years that prepares students to read, but is not all about getting ready for third grade tests!

CHAPTER SIX

HELP! WHAT TO DO FIRST, WHAT TO DO NEXT?

Now that you know what reading problems are, what causes them, and what struggling readers need, how do you get the right help for your child?

First: Get It In Writing

From the moment any concern is expressed by either you or someone at your child's school that he or she might have a reading problem, the child is protected under Section 504 of the Americans with Disabilities Act (ADA). This does not mean the school will suddenly spring into action and provide exactly what your child needs. It does mean that you and the school and district are now on notice that the child is struggling and needs help provided for under either the ADA's Individuals with Disabilities Education Act, or the still-evolving Response to Intervention protocol.

Your job at this moment is to get something in writing from the school's guidance counselor or your child's teacher that expresses the concern either from you or from them. When you ask for this documentation, your child's teacher may be reluctant to be explicit. Teachers might be discouraged, for instance, from recommending students for extra help, especially for Special Education services, because of the costs involved. (Costs to society down the road for struggling readers are far higher!) At the same time, in New York City, for instance, if a student's promotion is in doubt, the school must send a letter to the parents to let them know. This in turn is supposed to trigger a meeting at the school to discuss what can be done to help the student. Indeed, one of the stipulations of the Americans with Disabilities Act, called "The Child Find Mandate,"[20] requires schools to seek out and identify students who are struggling. New York City's "promotion in doubt" letter is about as specific as many school districts are likely to get to meet this mandate.

It is in the context of this meeting, or the letter, or any other triggering mechanism your school has, that you should ask if a learning disability is suspected. If the teacher or school is reluctant to be specific, you may need to get them to state their concern explicitly. For instance you could ask "Are you saying you think my child has a learning disability?" Follow up the conversation with a letter or e-mail re-capping what was said so that a record has begun. Send a copy of the letter or e-mail to your child's guidance counselor as well. Struggling readers are entitled to help under ADA, IDEA, and Response to Intervention. Your job at this moment is to confirm that you know that your child is struggling, and that you will work with the school to ensure he or she gets appropriate help. This, in turn, puts the school on notice that it is expected to work with you, going forward, to get the appropriate help.

What should you do next? Learning that your child may have a learning disability is likely to be emotionally grueling. So too is what you will need to do to get that appropriate help. So for now —

> Don't get overly anxious;

> Don't blame your child, the teacher, the school, or yourself;

Instead, understand that your role, whether you are ready for it or not, is to be your child's primary advocate. This book was written to help you prepare for that role; many additional resources will help you to execute it.

CHAPTER SEVEN

WHO'S IN CHARGE HERE?

Once it has been established that your child is a struggling reader, one of the first things you may notice is that no one person seems to be actually "in charge" of making sure he or she gets appropriate help. One would think that, given the time that has elapsed since the Americans With Disabilities Act (ADA) and Individuals with Disabilities Education Act (IDEA) were passed, things would be up to speed by now. But they aren't, and, again, for one over-riding reason: Congress has failed to fully fund IDEA. That has left states and districts to work out for themselves how to implement an under-funded mandate ever since.

What is your role?

With no one person truly "in charge," think of yourself as the "general contractor" for making sure your child gets help. Just as a housing contractor pulls together all the workers and materials needed to get a house built, you will need to pull together the people, programs, and materials that will help your child succeed.

What form that help will take, and who exactly will pay for it, will depend not only on your advocacy, but on where you live and on what resources are available to you. By "resources" I mean time, tenacity, and money. If your household income is high, you will likely be able to pay out-of-pocket for appropriate help if it comes to that. If your household income is very low, you are likely to be eligible for legal aid organizations that will help you get what you need. Also, if your child is in a school with many students eligible for the federal free-lunch program, then Title 1 funding is probably also being provided to that school to help struggling students. However, whether those funds are spent on the best intervention practices available can vary widely.

For those in the middle income brackets, you may have the hardest time extracting help from "the system." Regardless of your income level or what your schools do or don't provide, you need to stay on top of what your child's needs are. You cannot assume the right help will be provided at the right time without a lot of oversight from you and your "team."

That is why it is important to be fore-warned and fore-armed. Having to figure everything out from scratch for yourself and your child takes unnecessary time, energy, and money, and leaves your child struggling longer than necessary. To keep that from happening, your focus should be to:

> Learn as much as you can;
>
> Lean on other resources as much as you need to;
>
> Find the experts who can help you;
>
> Work with those experts to find the programs that will work best for your child.

What is the School's Role?

As I described in Chapter 6, as soon as you and the school have gone "on record" that your child is a struggling reader, the school is supposed to partner with you to help you find appropriate help.

However, since IDEA is *not* fully funded, school districts are under enormous pressure to try to contain costs. So you cannot assume that the school is going to be totally forthcoming about what you should do, or about where and how to get help. An elementary school teacher in New York City told me the principal of her school has told teachers to not even use the word "dyslexia" with parents. That, despite the fact that there are probably 5-6 dyslexics in every class in that principal's school! They are in addition to another 5-6 struggling readers per class who may have never learned, for instance, proper de-coding skills.

In my case, I was told by the guidance office of my older son's elementary school that "help from the outside" is usually better than what the school would be able to offer. It was not until years later, long after I'd found that help, and my son was flourishing, that I realized what parents-who-know-the-ropes do is to move quickly towards an "impartial hearing," between themselves and the New York City Department of Education to try to get appropriate help paid for as soon as they know help is needed. This cuts both ways, however. That might have taken a longer time, and there was no guarantee ahead of time that the DOE would have paid for the program we needed. While it was expensive, the help my sons got was exactly what they needed, when they needed it.

In 2009 the U.S. Supreme Court ruled[21] that parents can place their special needs children in private schools and then sue their local school districts for tuition. Before that, families had to try out public schools first, then sue if appropriate services or accommodations were not being provided.

This provision helps families move quickly to get their children into settings they believe are appropriate. However, families must pay tuition costs upfront, then wait to get reimbursed once their case is resolved. This solution is prohibitively expensive for most families.

What is Society's Role?

Families at high-income levels might be able to manage private-school tuition costs up-front. Families at low-income levels who get legal aid services can get the tuition waived until their cases are settled. It is middle-income families who are likely to struggle the most with private school placements.

This is just one of many scenarios in which access to money affects access to getting appropriate help for struggling readers (and which in turn prompted me to form The Right to Read Project!). That guarantee of the right to read for our nation's schoolchildren is still very much ahead of us, not behind us!

While our family paid directly for our children's help out-of-pocket, I do not think it is fair or appropriate to expect families to take on these costs. It is an issue of equity. Learning disabilities are a part of life, cutting across all demographics of race, income, nationality, and education level. Meanwhile, compulsory education is national law. Between those two facts, providing appropriate help to our four out of ten struggling readers is of national concern, and should be paid for either through IDEA or through health insurance, or both. For now, no single governmental entity bears the responsibility for providing and paying for appropriate help. That help exists, it just isn't deployed evenly and fairly across states, districts and schools. To my mind, it is as much society's role to provide that help as it is to educate our children in general. Until we get there, however, individual families must do what they can to make sure their struggling readers are helped. It is when parents band together to push for appropriate support that we will start to see true change in providing this help.

CHAPTER EIGHT

ABC's OF IDEA

Knowing the terms that define learning disabilities and the laws that cover them is crucial to knowing how to proceed with getting help for your struggling reader. Even if not every term applies to your particular child or situation, it is important to know them in case you hear them being used in doctors' offices or school "support team" meetings. These definitions are ordered from more general "big-picture" terms, to specific ones related to how the "big picture" gets implemented.

Americans with Disabilities Act (ADA)

Passed by Congress in 1990, the ADA is a civil rights law that protects people with disabilities from discrimination in workplaces, schools and other settings. The law was expanded in 2008 as the Americans with Disabilities Act Amendments Act, providing even greater reach to disabled persons. While ADA protects civil rights, no funding is attached to it to help states and school districts implement the law. (For details on ADAAA and its implications, see Note[22] in "References" at the end of this book.)

Section 504 of The Rehabilitation Act of 1973 ("Section 504")

The Rehabilitation Act of 1973 was the original law prohibiting discrimination against the disabled, preceding ADA by nearly two decades. It grew out of civil rights legislation of the 1960's forbidding discrimination based on race, creed and sex.

Section 504 of the Rehabilitation Act prohibits schools receiving federal funding from discriminating against students with disabilities. According to U.S. government guidelines:[23]

> "Section 504 states that 'no qualified individual with a disability in the United States shall be excluded from, denied the benefits of, or be subjected to discrimination under any program or activity that either receives Federal financial assistance or is conducted by any Executive agency or the United States Postal Service." (For a link to "Parent's Guide to Section 504 in Public Schools" see Note[24] for wrightslaw.com in "References" at the end of the book.)

The Individuals with Disabilities Education Act (IDEA)

IDEA was originally passed in 1975 as the Education for All Handicapped Children Act (EHA). It has been amended several times, with the most comprehensive changes being made in 2004. That law is called the Individuals with Disabilities Improvement Act of 2004, but in general people still refer to it as IDEA. According to federal guidelines:

> The Individuals with Disabilities Education Act (IDEA) is a law ensuring services to children

with disabilities throughout the nation. IDEA governs how states and public agencies provide early intervention, special education and related services to more than 6.5 million eligible infants, toddlers, children and youth with disabilities.

Infants and toddlers with disabilities (birth-2) and their families receive early intervention services under IDEA Part C. Children and youth (ages 3-21) receive special education and related services under IDEA Part B.[25]

"IDEA Part B" is where funding for these services is addressed. However, as I've mentioned, IDEA has never been fully funded by Congress, hence, the difficulty parents often have getting schools, districts and states to pay for the sorts of reading interventions their struggling readers need. Nevertheless, with or without adequate funding, your child is still protected by this law. That means that certain protections are in place that will help your child. In some states, that help extends to financing the sorts of reading interventions your child needs within the school, and without much fuss. In others, that help is not available unless you sue for it. In still others, help is available, but may not be the kind your child needs, leaving you to either sue for appropriate help, or to get it on your own outside of the school system.

Regardless of whether effective reading interventions are provided by your school or district, your child is entitled to them, and to the protections that having a learning disability confers under IDEA, ADA, and Section 504. This is important to know early on to help safeguard your child, for instance, from being "retained," or held back a grade, when what they really need is specialized help and/or testing accommodations. That is why it is crucial to get it in writing when your child's reading struggles are first flagged.

Free Appropriate Public Education (FAPE)

ADA and IDEA guarantee to each student in the U.S. a "free and appropriate education" regardless of race, creed, color, and disability. For learning disabled students, it does not always mean that the best education or supports will be found in the nearest public school. Depending on the nature of the disability, some school districts pay private school tuition for students whose needs cannot be met in a public school setting.

Least Restrictive Environments (LRE)

Disabled students are entitled to be educated in environments as close to a normal classroom setting as their disability will allow. Struggling readers can usually ultimately thrive in a regular classroom, as long as they receive appropriate reading interventions, and have supports in place. The latter might include having directions read aloud in early grades, large-format tests, or extended time on tests.

Special Education ("Special Ed")

"Special Education" refers to the programs and services that support disabled students under IDEA, as well as to the federal funding that supports those services. It is important to understand this pairing because it is through this funding stream that you are most likely to get payment for the services your child needs. Those services will be spelled out under the child's "IEP."

Individual Education Plans ("IEPs")

You and your medical and educational "team" will arrive at the specific type or types of remediation, modifications, and accommodations your struggling reader needs. These are then written into your child's "Individual Education Plan," or IEP. Remediation will be the reading "intervention(s)" specified by your practitioners. "Modifications" that may be put in place refer to alterations in the curriculum that might be needed while your child is being helped. "Accommodations" refer to physical alterations such as seating your child in the front of the classroom, use of a keyboard, or extended time on tests. (For comprehensive details and questions about IEPs, check out wrightslaw.com.[26])

Section 504 Accommodation Plans ("504s")

Accommodation Plans under Section 504 are often used more for behavioral disorders, or for making sure medications can be taken at school, than for learning disabilities. For learning disabled students, these plans are often what remain in place after a student has achieved enough remedial success to be declassified from Special Education. The 504 Accommodation Plan can be used to continue, for instance, testing accommodations such as extended time. Be aware that learning-disabled students continue to be protected under Section 504 whether or not a plan is in place. However, if you want to continue accommodations that a child had under an IEP, you will have to specifically ask and arrange for a 504 Plan. If you and your team expect your child will need extended time on high-stakes high school and college entrance exams, plan on keeping either an IEP or 504 Plan in place continuously that provides this accommodation.

Parents who decide to get all the help their children need outside of the school and outside of Special Education referrals can also use 504 Accommodation Plans for their children, as long as they are signed off on by qualifying practitioners. The school then needs to concur with the plan and sign off on it for it to be enforceable.

An important distinction is that if you think you are going to want or need your school district to provide (and pay for) services, the Special Education with IEP route is the one you should follow. (A full description of Section 504 can be found at greatschools.org.)[27]

Learning Disabilities (LD or L/D)

The National Institute of Child Health and Human Development (NICHD) gives what I consider the clearest explanation of learning disabilities that I have come across:

> Learning disabilities are caused by a difference in brain structure that is present at birth and is often hereditary. They affect the way the brain processes information.

This processing is the main function involved in learning.

Learning disabilities can impact how someone learns to read, write, hear, speak, and calculate. There are many kinds of learning disabilities and they can affect people differently.

[They] do not reflect IQ (intelligence quotient) or how smart a person is. Instead, a person with a learning disability has trouble performing specific types of skills or completing a task.

[Learning disabilities are] not the same as mental or physical disabilities …

Children with learning disabilities cannot be identified on the basis of acuity (such as vision or hearing) or other physical signs, nor can they be diagnosed solely based on neurological findings. Learning disabilities are widely regarded as variations on normal development and are only considered disabilities when they interfere significantly with school performance and adaptive functions."[28]

The full explanation can be found at the NICHD website (Note[28] above). It is important to understand fully what learning disabilities are, what they are not, and how differently they can affect people, since these questions and issues are likely to come up frequently as you advocate for your child.

Related Services

If services are called for in an IEP, but the school does not provide those services on-site, parents can look for outside providers for them. These are called "related services." In many respects, if you have a good provider of appropriate reading interventions where you live, you may be better off using their services anyway. It is hard for schools to cover the full range of services right there in the building for every Special Ed need, so parents should look for the most appropriate services recommended by their "team." Whether those services are in the school or outside of it, if they are stipulated in the IEP, they should be paid for by the school district.

Response to Intervention (RTI)

In 2004 the NICHD developed a new protocol to address the needs of special education students. Up to that point, a "waiting to fail" model had been in place. Under that provision, students were referred to special education only when they were demonstrably behind in their work. In the case of reading, for instance, they needed to be two years behind by grade 3 in order to get help through special education. To expedite this process, NICHD proposed RTI as a way to provide more intensive help to readers as soon as they showed a need for it, starting in kindergarten.

LD/Online gives a good description of how RTI was incorporated into IDEA 2004 --

> In 2006, another change [to IDEA 2004] was made when final regulations were released for IDEA 2004. For years, schools were required to wait until a child fell considerably behind grade level before being eligible for special education services. Today, with the release of the final regulations of IDEA 2004, school districts are no longer required to follow this 'discrepancy

model,' but are allowed to find other ways to determine when a child needs extra help. This is being implemented throughout the country through a process called Response to Intervention.[29]

It is important to understand, however, that RTI is a protocol that is rolling out quite slowly, and is left to the states to implement. There are no "RTI police" to make sure the protocol and its standards are rolled out on a common timetable and with standardized practices. States are even allowed to choose whether to follow the RTI protocol or stay with the "discrepancy model," even though the latter has fallen into disrepute as a way to refer a student for a Special Ed evaluation for learning disabilities!

RTI is divided into three tiers of intervention: Tier 1 provides high-quality, research-based classroom reading instruction, screenings, and group interventions. Students not making expected progress are then addressed by Tier 2 "Targeted Interventions," usually in small-group settings. Students still struggling after these interventions are then supposed to be provided with

Tier 3 intensive, one-on-one interventions. If even those don't work, the student should then be given a comprehensive evaluation for Special Education. (A full description of RTI can be found at Note[30] in "References" at the end of the book.)

At any time during the RTI "tiered" process, which can easily extend over a full school year, parents can ask for a Special Education evaluation. They don't have to wait to "try out" the three tiers of RTI if they think the child will need specialized help in the end anyway. Also, RTI is primarily intended for kindergarten through 4th grade. Keep in mind, though, that struggling readers in any grade can and should ask for help either through RTI or a Special Ed evaluation.

Academic Intervention Services (AIS) and Other Local Terms

"AIS" is a term used in New York and New Jersey, for instance, to describe state funding for struggling students that is separate from federal Special Education funding through IDEA. Different states have different terms for these streams of funding, and different criteria for how they are dispensed.

Supplementary Education Services (SES) Tutoring

Supplementary Education Services were established under the 2002 No Child Left Behind (NCLB) law to provide after-school tutoring for children in schools that receive Title 1 funding. For the most part, these services are provided by commercial vendors, community-based organizations (CBOs) or in after-school programs in which the school's teachers do the tutoring. This tutoring is designed to support or supplement classroom work. However, by this point in the book you probably realize that if your child is a struggling reader, he or she needs stronger reading interventions than what has been provided in the classroom or that is designed to reinforce standard classroom practice.

So if you are in a Title 1 school, and the school-based support team first tries to direct you to SES tutoring services, explain that you want specialized reading interventions as provided under Response to Intervention. It could be that the school has actually lined up such RTI providers through SES, but make sure this is the case before signing up for SES tutoring. In general, the specialized help you are looking for will be covered by AIS funding or Special Ed funding, not SES funding.

In any case, again, you are entitled to ask for a Special Education evaluation at any point in your child's schooling. You do not need to go through the various tiers of RTI first, if it appears that your child is going to need the Tier 3 multi-sensory interventions that, in your state, may only be available through an IEP.

CHAPTER NINE

YOUR ACTION PLAN

The preceding chapters have provided you with explanations of reading difficulties, background information, and definitions. Now what do you do with all of that information? What follows in this chapter and the next are a timeline and framework of actions you will need to take to get your child from struggling to successful reader. Not every action or situation may pertain to your particular child. Some of these actions may get collapsed together, or spread apart, depending on what you work out with your school, and what your school support team and your personal team of experts recommends.

Action Timeline

You learn your child is not reading on grade level. You follow up with your child's teacher and guidance counselor, in writing (Chapter 6), that you understand your child is struggling with reading, you suspect a learning disability, and you want him or her to get extra help. Your child is now recognized as protected under Section 504 of ADA, the Americans With Disabilities Act. (You can include that in your letter.)

1. Get vision and hearing tests NOW. You might discover that all your distracted, non-reading child needed were glasses, and your search might very well end here. Or he or she might turn out to be hearing impaired. Not all schools test vision and hearing, plus these tests will be more targeted and comprehensive than what your child is likely to get either in school or in annual physicals with his or her pediatrician.

2. Early on, ask the school to give your child the Grey Oral Reading Test (GORT). This is a relatively short test that is several decades old, and

so has stood the test of time. It will give a baseline for where your child's reading level is in relation to current grade level and to students throughout the country. If the school cannot or will not give the test, find an outside learning specialist who will. This test will not form a diagnosis on its own, but will help get everyone on the same page as to your child's reading level.

3. You and the School Support Team discuss what help can be offered by the school, and what sort of testing the school will provide. You accept or reject the school's help.

4. If you have accepted the school's psycho-educational testing, your child proceeds with that. When the results come in, if you do not agree with them, you can reject them and ask for an outside evaluation. In that case, the school district pays for the outside evaluation as well.

5. Alternatively, you can bypass the school's testing and proceed with private testing (usually neuro-psychological tests), but in that case you will be responsible for any payments. Some in-

surers cover these tests, so be sure to check ahead. Some only cover the tests if the child was first seen by, and then referred by, a neurologist.

6. Whichever of these routes you follow, the psycho-educational test by the school, or a neuro-psychological test with a private practitioner (or both), becomes the "baseline" on which treatment will be built.

7. The psycho-ed or neuro-psych evaluations test for "organic" brain difficulty in processing information, and establish grade-level equivalents for various academic skills. Results for specific skills can range from close together to far apart, and close to or far from the child's current grade level. Widely divergent results – for instance advanced math skills and below-grade reading skills – are considered "scattered," and are not at all unusual in children found to have learning disabilities.

8. Tests for expressive/receptive language ability that are conducted either by the school, or by the outside practitioner, are what usually indicate difficulties in reading. Remember, however, that

these evaluations do not specifically test for dyslexia.

9. By now, if no conspicuous or organic problem has been found, the various practitioners may recommend testing for ADD/ADHD, and/or for psychological issues such as anxiety. You can certainly go ahead with checking for these, but there are a few things to keep in mind. One is that symptoms for ADD/ADHD and for learning disabilities can look similar,[31] especially to teachers with many children in their classrooms. (This issue is addressed very well by Ronald D. Davis in the opening chapters of his book *The Gift of Dyslexia*.[32]) Also, children diagnosed with ADD/ADHD are often found to have learning disabilities instead of, or in addition to, any attentional disorder. Another possibility is that "inattentive" students are actually under-challenged. About.com describes how these varying conditions can be confused with attention disorders:

> Similar to a person with ADHD, someone with a learning disability may struggle with issues of attention and have difficulty

processing, organizing, remembering and learning information. Learning disabilities in reading, written language, and mathematics can all interfere with academic functioning, as can speech and language impairments and auditory and visual processing disorders. ADHD and specific learning disorders often occur together, but they are separate conditions.

A child who is gifted academically and is not challenged within the classroom may even display behaviors that are similar to ADHD as he or she becomes bored with the curriculum -- becoming inattentive, and/or impatient and disruptive. Along these same lines, a poor educational fit, or a classroom with a pervasive negative climate, a non-stimulating, un-motivating curriculum, or ineffective classroom management, all can lead to behaviors that look like, but may be unrelated to, ADHD.[33]

So it is well to make sure that a child has no learning disabilities before treating a diagnosis of ADD/ADHD, which generally involves medication.

10. Auditory Processing Disorder (APD, also known as CAPD for `Central Auditory Pro-

cessing Disorder) testing – this is a test you should definitely include before assuming you have the whole story on your child's learning abilities. Up to this point, you have been following the typical "screening" protocol. But because APD is something of an "orphan" condition – not as well-known as others cited here, and not easily diagnosed if practitioners are not nearby – you might end up hearing about it only in this book! Tests for APD are different from tests for "peripheral hearing," which you will have already had tested by an audiologist. Auditory processing refers to "what we do with what we hear." Through a detailed series of subtests, administered through headphones, audiologists who specialize in this field are able to determine whether sounds are being processed in a child's brain properly. There is enough overlap between some of the auditory processing disorders and dyslexia that the term "auditory dyslexia"[34] is used to describe this condition.

11. By now you should know whether or not your child has a learning disability that is affecting his or her reading. As you can see from the foregoing actions, there is no one test that specifically identifies dyslexia. Instead, just about every other possibility is ruled out. With no other conspicuous disability in play, your team should now be able to determine whether your child needs reading interventions available under "Tier 3" of Response to Intervention (RTI, Ch. 8 and 10).

At this point you will need to decide whether to pursue an IEP or 504 Accommodation plan. The diagnosing practitioners should be able to guide you on whether the school can provide enough services, or whether you will need to find them outside of the school. Keep in mind that if you want or need the school district to provide this help within the school, pay for it as a "Related Service," or send your child to a school that specializes in learning disabilities, you will need to have an IEP through the Special Education referral process.

CHAPTER TEN

YOUR PLAN IN ACTION

Getting your "Action Plan" into real action can extend over a period that can easily take up to two years. That, as I mentioned earlier, is if you're staying on top of things every step of the way! That was the timeframe in which I had worked, though nothing I was doing was anything I had planned ahead of time. All of this was completely new to me. I was not following any particular "game plan," but was following leads at the suggestions of every school or district official, clinician or fellow parent who had one. Having spent the better part of two decades writing market reports, I had learned to not hang up the phone with one person I was interviewing until I knew who was the next person I should speak to in order to get to the bottom of whatever I was researching at that moment. For this particular "research project," I was also driven by anxiety over a situation I knew nothing about, and by not wanting to let my son fall behind over some unexplained piece of this strange new puzzle that I might fail to understand.

By putting the various pieces of the puzzle together, I learned a lot very quickly, and got him to the help he needed much sooner than I might have if I had followed the usual school- and district-based protocol then in place. In fact, in the years since then, I have met many parents who had followed that protocol whose children were still not getting adequate help. I've met parents who had successfully used Impartial Hearings with the Department of Education for private school placements in schools for learning disabilities, for instance, but whose children were still not reading on grade level many years later! That, while programs exist that can bring struggling readers to grade level within weeks or months. One mother finally transferred her 8th grader, still not reading, to a different school and he was reading within three months!

Accessing Appropriate Help

The right help for struggling readers is out there. It does not need to be "invented." It just needs to be accessed. An emeritus member of the New York State Board of Regents, Adelaide Sanford, put it perfectly at a forum I attended a few years ago: "We don't have an 'achievement gap,' we have an 'access gap.'" As the "general contractor" for your child's success, you need to be in charge of "accessing" the right help!

Earlier, in defining ADA and IDEA, I described how these laws protect your struggling reader, but do not provide enough funding to help them. Hence the difficulty in getting schools, districts and states to pay for the sorts of specialized reading interventions that your child likely needs. Even so, your child is still protected by these laws. In some states that protection extends to financing the reading interventions your child needs within the school, and without much fuss. In others, that protection is not available unless you pursue due process hearings, or ultimately sue for it. In still others, help is available, but may not be the kind your child needs. That leaves you to either sue for it, or to get it on your own outside of the school system.

    Put another way, regardless of whether effective reading interventions are provided by your school or district, your child is entitled to them, and to the protections that having a learning disability confers. This is important to know early on to help safeguard your child, for instance, from being "retained," or held back a grade, when what they really need is specialized help and/or testing accommodations. That is why it is crucial to get it in writing (Chapter 6) as soon as your child's reading struggles first become known.

In the previous chapter I gave a timeline of actions you will likely need to follow in order to get your child to the right help. Again, if the issue is nearsightedness, for instance, you'll find that out early, and a pair of glasses may be the end of your particular child's reading struggles. If the issue is dyslexia, on the other hand, you will likely need to go through every step I outlined, and still have trouble getting the right help for your child in an expeditious timeframe. Why is that?

Even as more and more has become known about reading disabilities over the past two decades, state education departments and the US Department of Education (USDOE) have increasingly pushed back against referrals to Special Education. One reason is that, as I've mentioned, IDEA has never been fully funded, leaving individual states and school districts to make up the difference. Another reason is that, as USDOE often notes, most referrals to Special Education are for reading difficulties. Therefore, the thinking goes, if reading difficulties are addressed early, the need for Special Education services will be lessened. To that end, districts, states and USDOE are increasingly working into their instructional strategies Response to Intervention (RTI).

How Is RTI Implemented?

In 2004 the reauthorization of IDEA incorporated the NICHD's proposed new protocol to address the needs of special education students. Up to that point, the "waiting to fail" model had been in place, where students were referred to Special Education only after they were years behind in their work. To expedite this process, NICHD proposed RTI as a way to provide more intensive help to readers as soon as they showed a need for it, starting in kindergarten.

While RTI seems like a genuine improvement in addressing reading difficulties compared to "waiting to fail," the way it is playing out from state to state and classroom to classroom is widely variable. That is in part because it is left up to the states to decide how they will implement RTI. A second reason is that, again, most remediation funding follows Special Education referrals, so getting help through RTI will not automatically mean your child is being offered the help that will work best for him or her.

Congress has put aside a portion of Special Education funding to support RTI programs. In New York State, for instance, this funding supports Academic Intervention Services, which in turn support Tier 1 and Tier 2 RTI interventions. To get to Tier 3 interventions recommended in the International Dylsexia Association Matrix[35] in New York State, however, the state legislature has determined that a child must be referred to Special Education for an IEP, which will then pay for those services.

In the meantime, schools are encouraged to provide what help they can before such a referral is made. If the child's reading is improving and reaches grade level, it is assumed that an appropriate level of RTI has been reached, and the interventions can stop.

This may be fine for struggling readers who need help only with decoding skills, for instance. For dyslexics, on the other hand, it is not likely to be enough. Most will need "Tier 3" interventions, and the sooner the better. These are where the intensive, multi-sensory programs are found that will best help them learn to read.

As you can see, you will need to be informed about and involved in decisions made about using RTI in the classroom, or as "pull-out services," right from the beginning. Don't assume the school will have you in this "loop" from the beginning, however! After all, schools are trying to avoid Special Ed referrals, so they may want to try as many RTI interventions as they have on hand before alerting you to a possible learning disability. Meanwhile, your child could have what might be considered a "false positive" for reading improvement through RTI. A year or two later he or she may be struggling all over again because the problem was really something quite different from what the RTI intervention was addressing. It is much better for your child to be properly diagnosed and remediated early on!

Finally, RTI was arrived at by NICHD, the U.S. Congress (via IDEA), and the U. S. Department of Education to address struggling readers. However, Congress has left it up to states to implement, which in turn often leave it up to individual districts. In New York City, for example, the choice of RTI/Academic Intervention Services programs is left to individual principals. They in turn leave implementation of the programs to early-grade teachers, who are often the newest, youngest and least-experienced in the school.

While RTI promises a great advance over "waiting to fail," its success as a full-grown, full-blown array of interventions for struggling readers is still ahead of us. In the meantime, your role as your child's "general contractor" can help you steer your child to appropriate help.

How Do I Know if RTI is working?

A sure sign that a reading intervention is working is, of course, improved reading skills! However, to avoid the possibility of "false positives," you should cross-check with members of your team. Follow-up reading tests different from those related to the actual intervention can give you and the school a better idea of how well the intervention is working.

Other signs of a successful intervention are that the child is more relaxed, enjoying school more, and/or is spending less time on homework and is more able to do it by him- or herself.

How Do I Know if My Child Needs Special Education Services?

If you, school officials, or members of your team see that your child is not progressing with RTI, then it is time to pursue a Special Education referral. Again, you do not have to wait through all three levels of RTI to do this if you, or your team, think those interventions will not be enough.

Getting help through Special Education does not automatically mean a child is sent to a separate classroom with children of widely different needs, overseen by a teacher who can't possibly accommodate all those needs at once. However, this is often the vision parents have of Special Ed, and a big reason they try to avoid having their children referred to it. Keep in mind that parents have to sign off on an IEP, so if there are provisions with which you disagree, you are entitled to contest them and have them replaced with provisions you and your team consider appropriate.

In a Special Education referral, you, your medical and educational team, and the school will arrive at the specific type or types of remediation your struggling reader needs. These are then written into your child's IEP.

Who Initiates Referrals to Special Education?

A referral to Special Education can be initiated either by a school or by parents. When it is initiated by parents, the school must comply with testing the student for learning disabilities. When a Special Ed referral is initiated by the school, it is optional for parents to comply. When it is initiated by a teacher, it is up to the principal to decide whether a referral will be pursued. If a teacher has initiated a referral, the principal has denied it, but parents want to pursue it, the school must comply.

Who Conducts the Special Education Testing?

As I described earlier, a Special Ed evaluation can be conducted entirely through the school, entirely through outside providers, or a combination of the two. The last scenario is common in New York State, for instance, when a parent thinks a school evaluation has fallen short. If parents disagree with the school's evaluation, they can appeal to the district to pay for an outside evaluation. Both evaluations involve a psycho-educational, or a neuro-psychological battery of tests which becomes the baseline on which to build an IEP. Here's the problem: neither evaluation specifically picks up dyslexia. As I also mentioned earlier (Ch. 9), what these tests do is screen for everything else. Then, if no other disability presents itself, it can be deduced that there is a reading disability. As Dr. Sally Shaywitz explains, dyslexia is --

> "a reading difficulty in a child or adult who otherwise has good intelligence, strong motivation, and adequate schooling."….[Its diagnosis] reflects a reading difficulty that is

unexpected for a person's age, intelligence, level of education, or profession. It is a clinical diagnosis based on a thoughtful synthesis of information – from the child (or adult's) personal and family history; from observations of her speaking and reading; and from tests of reading and language. As in other conditions in medicine, the history is the most critical component and is afforded the most respect.... The tests that are ultimately selected must be chosen with great care." (*Overcoming Dyslexia*, by Sally Shaywitz, p. 132.)[36]

For this reason, you are likely to want to question a school evaluation, no matter what it finds, and go outside of the school for people who are expert in diagnosing dyslexia or other reading disabilities. In effect, dyslexia is often the diagnosis that is left after no other possible reason for delayed reading can be found. That means no organic problems with the brain, no vision or hearing problems, no emotional trauma. All of these have to be ruled out before dyslexia is even entertained by many school systems as a possible diagnosis. Note also how much the beginning of Dr. Shaywitz's description parallels those of Kerr and Morgan (pages 12-13) more than 100 years ago!

What If I Don't Agree With the IEP?

Going through the referral process does not mean you have to accept an IEP if you do not agree with it. At the same time, if you refuse an evaluation or an IEP, *and* you do not look for any help outside of the school, *and* the school has already tried some form of remediation that has not helped, it is likely that your child may start to be held back, or "retained." This is not necessarily because the school is being mean, but because, again, the money that pays for much of the extra help beyond classroom practices or preliminary Response to Intervention programs is provided through Special Education funding.

Again, once you and the school are on notice with each other that your child is struggling, he or she is protected under Section 504 of ADA. However, if you end up rejecting all forms of help the school offers, and do not seek outside help, then you are tying the school's hands in terms of its ability to help your child. Remedial efforts at whatever grade or level of need entail something of a "dance" between the school and the family in order to arrive at what will work best for your child. If you are not contributing to your side of the "dance," the school can only do so much on its own.

What If the IEP isn't Helping -- How To Get From "Wrong" Help to "Right" Help

If the provisions written into your child's IEP turn out to be not working, your recourse is to have the IEP revised to include other measures that will help. These would be arrived at in consultation among you, your team and the school. It is possible that you might go through the whole referral process, get an IEP, and your child starts to get help, but it is not necessarily the right kind of help. That is why it is crucial to educate yourself about this whole process as much as possible. You don't have to be an "instant expert" on every remediation program, but you need to know what it takes to access the one(s) your child needs. Part of accessing that help is working with clinicians (and lawyers if necessary) whom you trust, and whose diagnoses square with what you're seeing and experiencing in your child's struggles. For instance, a classic example of what can happen is that a teacher is concerned that a child is not paying attention in class. You are advised to get testing for ADD/ADHD because it seems like an "attention" problem is the issue. However, as described earlier, many children look inattentive because they cannot read, or perhaps cannot screen out classroom noises enough to hear the teacher's voice, or cannot see the blackboard/whiteboard!

Lack of attentiveness might also be coming from a totally different direction. For instance, a child may be feeling distracted by personal problems such as bullying, or conflicts at home. Others, not sufficiently challenged by the classwork, may be "acting out" from boredom. Still other children are what is called "twice challenged" – they may have learning disabilities but also score at the high end on IQ measures, meaning they qualify for "gifted" education. That is why it is crucial to check for learning disabilities as part of any seeming "behavioral" or "attention" problems.

Keep in mind also that if your child is outperforming parameters set by an IEP, you can ask to have it revised to include more challenging work.

"IEPs" Versus "504s"

There are a range of reasons why parents and schools might want to forego the IEP process altogether. For schools, districts and states, it can be an expensive and labor-intensive process just to get to an IEP, and an even more expensive one to fulfill the requirements. This of course does not mean they are not obliged to fulfill those requirements, but it does explain why extracting help from "the system" is often so difficult.

Parents, meanwhile, might be reluctant to have their children "labeled" as "Special Ed" kids. So they may opt out of that whole process and instead work with their "support team" to arrive at a diagnosis and interventions that fit and that work. These in turn entitle children to Section 504 accommodations. It is crucial to remember, however, that the money that is attached to IDEA Special Education funding is NOT automatically attached to a 504 Accommodation plan. That means that while you can secure extended time on tests and other accommodations for your child, you cannot assume your district will pay for necessary reading interventions outside of what they would provide under an IEP. Some schools, states and districts might do this, but you need to check before coming to a final conclusion between an IEP versus a 504 Accommodation Plan.

In either case, the school may encourage you to "try out" the various levels of RTI the school has implemented before being evaluated for Special Education services or implementing a 504 Plan. Unless you are in a school system that has a highly-evolved RTI protocol, however, you cannot assume, at least at the time of this writing, that your child will have access to the higher levels of help that he or she might need. Keep in mind that you are legally entitled to skip RTI and go right to a Special Ed referral if you and your team think that is what is needed.

For all of these reasons, some parents forego the whole IEP process and find help outside of the school system altogether. For their children, 504 Accommodation Plans are developed among the reading intervention providers, a licensed professional (it could be the child's pediatrician if the intervention providers are not licensed), and the school support team. I did this, but frankly, it was because I didn't know any better. Like many parents, I was concerned about "labeling." I also thought that since the reading program we used worked so well, there was no need to pursue an IEP. However, we would have stood a much better chance of getting reimbursed for the reading program if we had used an IEP. (For a good description of variations among these laws, see "Key Differences Between Section 504, the ADA and the IDEA" at Wrightslaw.com.[37])

"Supports" in IEPs and 504 Accommodation Plans

A major component of either an IEP or a 504 Accommodation Plan is spelling out what sorts of special supports or accommodations your child will need as he or she goes through an intervention program, and after it is over.

"Accommodations" cover physical adjustments such as where a child might need to sit in a classroom (close to a teacher if screening out surrounding noise is an issue, for example) to extra time on tests. Testing accommodations can also include a quiet, separate setting for testing, or having directions read aloud. Accommodations reflect a student's current level of functioning. A student just starting to get help will likely need more intensive accommodations than one who has gotten help and now just needs specific supports to keep up with classwork.

"Modifications" are adjustments to the curriculum that might be needed. In the case of struggling readers, this could mean a reduced number of pages to be read per day or per week, or a reduced homework load. As the student's reading skills strengthen, the need for such modifications will likely lessen. However, the need for extra time on tests should always be included as an accommodation for dyslexic readers.

Why Extra Time for Testing?

To people not familiar with testing accommodations, extra time on tests can seem like an advantage for learning-disabled students. Actually, what it does is "level the playing field" with their non-disabled peers, according to Dr. Sally Shaywitz of Yale. In an interview she explained:

> "... there is a neurobiological difference between dyslexic and non-impaired readers: not in intelligence, but in the systems that allow you to read rapidly. The neural system allowing rapid, fluent reading in typical readers is disrupted in dyslexic readers. As a result the dyslexic reader cannot call upon the neural circuitry for rapid reading and must read slowly."[38]

On the question of whether extra time on tests poses an unfair advantage, in her book *Overcoming Dyslexia*, Dr. Shaywitz explains:

"Researchers have compared the performance of learning-disabled and non-learning-disabled college students on timed and untimed standardized tests. The results were consistent: Only students diagnosed as learning-disabled actually showed a significant improvement in test scores with additional time." (p.337)

Dr. Jay Lucker of Gallaudet University, an expert in diagnosing auditory processing disorders, explained the difference between regular and impaired readers to me this way: "You can get from mid-town Manhattan to New Jersey through the Midtown Tunnel (the most direct route), or you could go downtown, take the Brooklyn/Battery Tunnel, then the Verazzano Bridge to Staten Island, and eventually end up in New Jersey. The first route is more direct, but the second route might be more interesting. Both will get you to New Jersey."

Struggling readers may need more time to get through tests, and to process language in general. At the same time, that doesn't mean they don't have many other strengths, and their minds may have many interesting stops along the way from Point A to Point B.

As to having directions read aloud, younger children are likely to be familiar with the language used to test reading skills and comprehension on standardized tests, but not with the more formal language of instructions, for instance. For that reason, you may want to include "have test directions read aloud" on standardized tests for struggling readers in elementary school. Early on, we even had the accommodation say "have directions read aloud twice." It helped!

Homework Accommodations

Homework time can become a battleground even in families without struggling readers. That has much to do with the "homework explosion" of the past two decades. Students of all ages are now being asked to do far more homework than were their parents. (More on homework in Chapter

11.) For IEPs and 504 Plans, consider including accommodations such as letting your child type homework, modifying the actual amount of homework such as fewer math problems, dictating essays in early grades, etc. For instance, if your child does well in math and the teacher is giving twice the number of problems that can reasonably be called "practice," then try to work into the IEP or the 504 plan modifications that allow a reduction in math homework "so that the child can focus on reading." More experienced teachers (not to mention those who have children of their own!) often give less homework than younger or less-experienced teachers.

    Think of homework accommodation requests purely in terms of time, and then present it that way. Extra time on testing, for instance, is about "processing speed," not intelligence. Your child is simply using different neural pathways. If a child needs extra time to get through a class-wide test, then it stands to reason that a reduced homework load will similarly "level the playing field," bringing it into line with the amount of time that non-struggling readers are spending on their homework. School should not be endless punishment for having a learning disability, but a place where all types of learners can succeed. Struggling readers need the right help and supports, and the right types of work, not more time on the wrong kinds of help or schoolwork.

Start Early on Accommodations for the SAT and ACT

Over the past few decades, there was something of an "explosion" of high school juniors being diagnosed with learning or behavioral problems that called for extended time on tests. Before long, it was becoming clear that these diagnoses were coinciding with students needing to take college entrance exams. To sort out these newly diagnosed students from those with long-term IEPs and 504 plans, the College Board and the ACT (American College Testing) have become much stricter in their requirements for extended time on the SAT and the ACT. This is another reason to pursue an IEP for struggling readers for the long-term, even if it converts to a 504 Plan by high school. Whether you are using an IEP or a 504 Plan, both the College Board and ACT expect them to have been in place over, minimally, the previous three years of a student's schooling. In addition, they will expect updated diagnostic testing to have been done within the prior three years of your request for accommodations.

Making sure your child meets these requirements should begin as soon as your child starts high school, since many schools give the PSAT in tenth grade as well as eleventh grade. Starting early will also give you time in case you have to appeal an adverse decision on extended time. Make sure your child makes use of extra time on tests as needed throughout high school, as the College Board and ACT include actual use of accommodations in their considerations as well.

Encourage Self-Advocacy

Don't assume your child will be ready to advocate for him- or herself until middle school at the earliest, and more likely not until high school. By that time, having your parent even show up at school can be a source of mortification, so they are likely to step up to the challenge just so that you won't show up to do it for them!

It is hard to expect a third-grader to remind teachers that they should have extra time on a test. However, in middle school, and especially by high school, students who need extra time should make sure they make use of it. Often it means going to a separate classroom for tests, or staying longer after the rest of the class has left, but if the practice has been in place for a long time, the student will be used to "the drill," as well as aware that he or she needs it. Also, they are unlikely to be alone in needing it, no matter how small their schools are!

If your high schooler has been provided extended time or other accommodations through an IEP or a 504 Plan and is not using them, you will likely need to show up at the school to find out why. You can do so at parent-teacher conferences, open school weeks, or through special appointments with teachers or guidance counselors to make sure everyone is on the same page about using extended time or other accommodations. Again, keep in mind that the College Board and ACT will want to know that extended time was actually used by students when they consider such requests for their tests.

CHAPTER ELEVEN

YOUR STRUGGLING READER

AT HOME

To help bring your child from struggling to successful reader, the actions you'll need to take may seem constant, and at times feel overwhelming. When you and your child are home together, it will be far more helpful for both of you if you try not to bring whatever feelings of frustration you may have from dealing with "the system" into your relationship. As much as possible, try to make home life a respite from your child's reading struggles, rather than a reminder of them.

Let Your Child "Get a Life!"

In the test-driven world that American schools have become in the early 21st century, parents might forget how different were their own childhoods. A great reminder comes from *The Centerburg Tales*, featuring zany stories in the small-town world of Homer Price. Published in 1943 by Robert McCloskey, author of other beloved books such as *Make Way for Ducklings*, this description of Homer's after-school activities reminds us that children can and should have interests and responsibilities beyond the schoolroom doors.

> "Homer's father owns a tourist camp. Homer's mother cooks fried chicken and hamburgers in the lunch room and takes care of the tourist cabins while his father takes care of the filling station. Homer does odd jobs about the place. Sometimes he washes windshields of cars to help his father, and sometimes he sweeps out cabins or takes care of the lunch room to help his mother.
>
> "When Homer isn't going to school, or doing odd jobs, or playing with other boys, he works on his hobby which is building radios. He

has a workshop in one corner of his room where he works in the evenings."[39]

While written in 1943, this profile is little different from the types of things most children were doing after school up until the "homework explosion" that began in the 1990's. If many decades-worth of children suffered no ill-effects from moderate amounts of homework and time to do chores plus explore their own interests, you can be sure your children won't either. In fact, brain research shows that out-of-school activities such as music lessons[40] enhance overall learning, even into old age! In addition, sleep[41] is vital to converting what children and adults learn from short-term[42] to long-term memory.

So rather than turn after-school time into yet more schoolwork, let your child develop interests, play with friends and siblings, help with housework, and otherwise see how the world works beyond the classroom.

This means making sure the time and resources are available for them to develop those interests, not that you have to run a personal out-of-school or after-school program for them. If after-school care is needed because no adults are home after school, look for programs that are not all about more schoolwork. If you cannot afford art, dance or music lessons, see if there are scholarships available where these classes are offered, or through your job, school or place of worship. Alternatively, you can trade off skills with other families, such as sewing for drawing, or cooking for music lessons, etc. Look for ways for your child to engage in hands-on play, full-body play, and to use materials and pursue activities that are different from what they find in school. Sports, of course, are a natural outlet for full-body play, and many schools, towns and cities offer free venues for that.

Homework: HELP!

If your child has a learning disability, it is even more important that, rather than come home to still more schoolwork disguised as homework, he or she get a chance to relax and do things that are NOT about school. "All work and no play makes Jack a dull boy" is for real! Extending the school day into full evenings of parent-supervised homework doesn't just make our children "dull" (as in tedious, not dumb!), it deprives them of time to develop their own interests. These interests often do more to inform what we will become as adults than does a lot of what we do in school! Let school take its proper place in your child's life as the source of his or her formal education, and as a vital resource to aid them towards adulthood. But try not to let schoolwork and homework consume every waking hour to the point of crowding out family life, outdoor play, and unstructured time that lets children pursue their own interests and learn how to interact with their peers and other adults outside of the classroom.

All that said, homework is a reality in most American schools. It just needs to be kept in perspective. The goal is to arrange things so that homework does not take over your family life, does not overwhelm your children, and especially so it does not "punish" them for being struggling readers. Guidelines[43] from the National Education Association and National PTA recommend that homework be limited to 10 minutes per night per grade. That means, for instance, that third-grade homework would be 30 minutes.

A "meta-analysis" of homework research[44] conducted by Harris Cooper of Duke University stands as the benchmark on the subject. He found that benefits of homework, in terms of improved academic achievement, did not actually kick in until *6th grade*. At that point, around age 11, children are able to be more self-sufficient about their homework. From 6th grade on, gradually increased amounts of homework correlated to improved academic achievement through high school, *up to a total of two-and-a-half hours in twelfth grade*. Many students are getting that much homework in *elementary* school!

Thus, more is not better in piling on the homework. If your child is in a school that gives excessive amounts of homework (i.e., more than the NEA/National PTA recommendation), incorporate into the IEP or 504 Plan modifications or accommodations that will allow for a reduced homework load (see Chapter 10).

Try to keep your child's homework confined to a fixed period of time. If it is not finished within that timeframe, close the books. Eventually he or she will either be able to stay focused for that period, or you may need to add homework accommodations or modifications into the IEP or 504 plan. Be sure to coordinate with your child's teacher as you go along so that incomplete homework does not become a reason for bad grades, losing recess time, or having your child repeat a grade!

Be mindful also that if homework drags on, and you're dragged into it nightly, your child may have figured out this is the only way he or she can get your undivided attention. I saw this happen with friends whose children had no learning problems! You can turn this dynamic around by offering to do something together *after* the homework is finished. You can say, for instance, "If you finish this by 8:30 then we'll have time to read/play a game/you can draw a picture ..."

whatever is special to your child before bedtime. Make sure you deliver!

If you are totally involved in your child's homework night after night (year after year?) then the school is probably not a good match.

If your child truly needs you by his or her side to get through homework in the early grades because reading skills are still shaky, then that may be necessary for the short-term. Longer-term, try to work something out so that you do not end up doing this for years on end! You can do that either through homework modifications or accommodations (Chapter 10), or by voting with your feet and finding a less pressured school. We did that, and it transformed our family life. Remember, homework is for the child, not for you!

If you do not have the patience to help with homework without things getting explosive, find someone who does – another adult, a sitter, a sibling, a cousin, or trade off with neighbors. It's important to not let this damage your relationship with your child.

If your child's school has an after-school program for supervised homework, you could consider using that. My own preference is for children at the elementary level to be playing after school while there is still daylight, whether at home or in a playground, in organized sports, or in after-school programs. Older children can be directed to more formal after-school activities such as music lessons, sports teams, or other programs where they can explore their interests.

If homework is such that you feel like you are semi-home-schooling your child, then it is simply too much. Work with other parents and with the school to try to bring it into line with the NEA/PTA guidelines of 10 minutes per grade per night. Your school's PTA could host a viewing and discussion of *The Race to Nowhere*,[45] an excellent documentary on this subject.

Most parents on both sides of the homework divide don't actually speak up. When I served on a homework policy committee for my school district, I was told for the umpteenth time that as many parents complain about too much homework as complain about too little. I asked the teacher and administrator on the committee how many parents actually spoke up, and they said only about 10 percent speaking for each side!

If circumstances with the school and with your child's trajectory of remediation are such that you feel like you are semi-homeschooling no matter what you do, you might want to take it on full-time, at least for a while. That way you can cover the same material you're probably covering anyway, and incorporate into your child's day other activities that you both want for him or her, but that are not happening between the school-day and homework time. If your child likes school well enough, and any "homework crisis" seems transitory – for instance, things were fine last year, but now it is problematic with the introduction of long division – then try to work through it. However, if you live in a district where homework is doled out relentlessly, the school is unresponsive, and a transfer (or moving!) is not an option, you may actually want to consider home-schooling, at least temporarily.

I know people who home-school, so, based on their experiences, can say I would ONLY recommend it if you know you are temperamentally suited for it, truly have the time, patience, and tenacity to see it through, and have a strong support system to help you do it right. If it becomes parking your child in front of "educational" television in early grades, or on-line classes in middle- or high school, this is not going to address his or her need for the kinds of hands-on learning and personal interaction most children love, and that struggling readers in particular need.

Ideally, social interactions in school are as integral to children's development as the actual learning. At the same time, parents need to do what is best for a particular child in any given moment. Keeping flexible about what is "best" as you proceed from kindergarten through 12th grade can help you make adjustments to your child's education, if you need to, as you go along.

CHAPTER TWELVE

CLOSING THOUGHTS

Don't Wait

When it comes to making sure your child's reading is on track, there is no point in waiting. As soon as a child is struggling with reading, help should be available. The child is not being "lazy" or dilatory, he or she just needs the right kind of help. When that help is given, your child will be on track, and you will have saved both of yourselves much anxiety and frustration.

To get to the right help, you have to be the strong one for your child, the advocacy "general contractor," as I described earlier. School systems are overwhelmed and underfunded. Early-grade teachers are often the least experienced. That is why it is important for you to find out as much as you can so you can get to the right help, and make sure your child gets that help.

You may feel completely alone with this at times. Spouses, siblings, friends, parents and in-laws with no experience of learning disabilities may be oblivious or even disparaging about what you are going through. Keep your focus, and surround yourself with people who can help and support you through this.

You are not alone – get with a group, even if it's online, or just one other parent to compare notes with on a park bench while your kids are at the playground.

Have a Support System

Your support system will include your "team" of practitioners, of course, but also find friends who understand what you are going through. For me, one was a friend who helped clarify what was being assigned for homework in elementary school almost every night – for years! Another friend and her husband, who works in Special Education, could explain details that the school would not or could not provide.

Check in on the "What Worked for Me" section of *The Right to Read Project* blog[46] – then come back and post what you find works for you, your child, and your family!

These first months and years will not be easy ones, but your efforts will make all the difference in helping your struggling reader to succeed.

RESOURCES

At the beginning you may feel overwhelmed by what needs to be done to help your struggling reader. So the following list provides resources to help you through the process. It is mostly comprised of resources I used, or that I heard about from other parents in relation to their children's reading struggles. Don't feel you have to take a year off just to read up on reading problems before you can do anything. Instead, get your plan of action in motion (Chs. 9 and 10), and use these resources as support along the way. Add whatever you find that works to your list of resources (and then share them on The Right to Read Project blog!)

Legal help

    International Dyslexia Association
    Wrightslaw.com
    Advocates for Children
    Local lawyers who specialize in educational advocacy
    Federal, state, city, county, or local education websites

Websites for Learning Disabilities

Some of these link directly to related articles in the "References" section. Once you are there, skip around the sites for additional information related to your questions or concerns.

    Wrightslaw.com
    GreatSchools.org
    LDonline.org
    ncld.org (National Center for Learning Disabilities)
    smartkidswithld.org
    dyslexia.yale.edu
    idea.ed.gov (US Dept. of Education)

nichd.nih.gov (National Institutes of Child Health and Human Development)

Books

Overcoming Dyslexia by Sally Shaywitz
The Gift of Dyslexia by Ronald D. Davis

Web-Browsing

Type in anything from single words to whole questions that you have along the way. If it's anywhere, it will likely be online! Once you are finished with the link you started with, skip around through the site to see if there is more material there that is relevant to your situation.

Materials

Explode the Code workbooks for phonetics and phonemic awareness
Clay for modeling letters (esp. for *The Gift of Dyslexia* program)
Three-dimensional letters and numbers
Math Help: abacus, blocks, Duplo, measuring cups, cut-outs, whatever manipu-

latives work for your child to help with math and, later, fractions.

Reading Intervention Programs

    Lindamood/Bell Learning Processes
    Davis Dyslexia Correction Services
    Orton-Gillingham and/or Wilson
    Fast-Forward

School-wide Programs

    Preventing Academic Failure (PAF)
    Reading Recovery
    Read 180 (for middle school and older)
    Success for All
    Wilson and Wilson Fundamentals

Many more programs are listed on the International Dyslexia Association's Matrix of Multi-Sensory Programs.[47]

REFERENCES

CHAPTER 2

1. (p. 6) -- http://www.nytimes.com/2007/12/05/business/worldbusiness/05iht- dyslex-ia.4.8602036.html?_r=2&

2. (p. 6) -- http://money.cnn.com/magazines/fortune/fort une ar-chive/2002/05/13/322876/index.html.

3. (p. 6) -- http://www.economist.com/node/215 56230

CHAPTER 4 –

4. (p. 11) -- http://www.nationalreadingpanel.org/publicati ons/publications.html

5. (p. 13) -- http://www.jstor.org/stable/994118?seq=9&

6. (p. 14) -- Wilder, Laura Ingalls. *On the Banks of Plum Creek.* New York: Harper Collins. 2004....(Orig. pub 1937) 352 pp

7. (p.17)–Re"The Wild Child"
   http://en.wikipedia.org/wiki/Jean_Marc_Gaspard_Itard

8. (p.20) – Shaywitz, Sally. *Overcoming Dyslexia*. Alfred A. Knopf: New York. 2003. 416 pp.

9. (p. 20) – http://www.google/search?q=dyslexic+brain&ie=utf-8%oe=utf-8&aq=t&rls=org.mozilla:en-US:official&client=firefox-a

10. (p.20) – http://news.bbc.co.uk/2/hi/health/4384414.stm

CHAPTER 5

11. (p.24) – http://www.nationalreadingpanel.org/Press/press_rel_4_13_00.htm and

12. (p.24) – http://www.nationalreadingpanel.org/NRPAbout/about_nrp.htm

13. (p.25) -- http://educationnext.org/the-reading-first-controversy/ (See also http://www.edexcellencemedia.net/publications/2008/200803_toogoodtolast/reading_first_030508.pdf)

14. (p.27) - - http://www.nrcld.org/resources/ldsummit/hallahan2.html

15. (p.27) – IBID

16. (p. 28) -- http://america-education.org/1463-orton-samuel-t-18791948.html

17. (p. 28) -- http://www.sciencedaily.com/releases/2003/05/030519083450.htm

18. (p. 29) -- The International Dyslexia Associations Matrix of Multi-Sensory Structured Language Programs - http://www.interdys.org/ewebeditpro5/upload/ MSL2007finalR1.pdf

19. (p. 32) The Right to Read Project blog http://righttoreadproject.org/

CHAPTER 6

20. (p. 37) – http://www.wrightslaw.com/blog/?p=49

CHAPTER 7:

21. (p. 43) -- http://www.nytimes.com/2009/06/23/education/23special.html

CHAPTER 8:

22. (p. 48) --) http://www.ncld.org/on-capitol- hill/federal-laws-aamp-ld/adaaa-a-section-504/americans-with-disabilities-act- amendments-act-adaaa

23. (p. 49) -- U.S. Government Guidelines on Section 504: http://www.ada.gov/cguide.htm

24. (p. 49) – http://www.wrightslaw.com/info/iep.index.htm

25. (p. 50) – http://idea.ed.gov/

26. (p. 53) – http://www.wrightlsaw.com/advoc/articles/iep_guidance.html

27. (p. 55) – Parent's Guide to Section 504 in Public Schools http://www.greatschools.org/special-education/legal-rights/868-section-504.gs

28. (p. 56) – http://www.nichd.nih.gov/health/topics/learningdisabilities.cfm (NOTE: this link is no longer accessible – the NICHD changed its website in Dec. 2012. However, I have kept the previous definition

in the text because, as I mentioned, it is the clearest I have yet come across. You can find other/additional material on NICHD.gov on learning disabilities.)

29. (p. 59) – http://www.ldonline.org/features/idea2004

30. (p. 60) – http://www.rtinetwork.org/learn/what/whatisrti

Chapter 9

31. (p.67) – http://blogs.edweek.org/edweek/speced/2011/07/a_new_report_from_the_1.html?cmp=ENL- EU-NEWS2

32. (p. 67) -- Davis, Ronald D with Eldon M. Braun. *The Gift of Dyslexia*. (Revised and Expanded in 2010.) Perigree Books.

33. (p. 68) - http://add.about.com/od/ evaluationanddiagnosis/a/Adhd-Like-Symptoms-But-Not-Adhd.html

34. (p. 69) -- http://www.ldonline.org/article/16285/Moncrieff, Auditory Dylsexia (from 2001.

Google "auditory dyslexia" or "Deborah Moncrieff" for much more on this issue).

CHAPTER 10:

35. (p. 77) -- The International Dyslexia Associations Matrix of Multi-Sensory Structured Language Programs - http://www.interdys.org/ewebeditpro5/upload/ MSL2007finalR1.pdf

36. (p. 83) – Shaywitz, Sally. *Overcoming Dyslexia.* (Cited at Note 8)

37. (p. 89) – "Key Differences Between Section 504, the ADA, and the IDEA by Peter Wright and Pamela Wright. http://www.wrightslaw.com/info/sec504.summ.rights.htm

38. (p.91) – Dyslexia and the Americans With Disabilities Amendment Act: a Q&A with Dr. Sally Shaywitz. http://dylsexia.yale.edu/Policy_QA.html

CHAPTER 11

39. (p.101) McCloskey, Robert. "The Case of the Sensational Scent," (p.10), *Centerburg Tales.* New York: The Viking Press. 1943. (149 pp.)

40. (p. 101) – http://www.positscience.com/blog/2011/04/20/music-lessons-in-childhood-boost-brain-performance/

41. (p. 101) – http://www.schoolfamily.com/blog/2011/08/16/children-sleep-and-long-term-memory

42. (p. 101) – http://www.scientificamerican.com/article.cfm?id=experts-short-term-memory-to-long-term&page=2%20

43. (p. 104) NEA/PTA guidelines – (c. 2002-2012) http://www.nea.org/tools/16938.htm

    Plus for current (as of 2013) national debate on this exact issue of ten minutes per night per grade,(even though the NEA/PTA seemed to have settled it by 2002!) see http://222.huffingtonpost.com/vicki-abeles/national-homework guide-lines_b_1568899.html

44. (p.104) -- http://today.duke.edu/2006/09/homework_op ed.html

45. (p.107) -- http://www.racetonowhere.com/

CHAPTER 12

46. (p.113) -- The Right to Read Project blog
http://righttoreadproject.org/

RESOURCES

47. (p.118) The International Dyslexia Associations Matrix of Multi-Sensory Structured Language Programs - http://www.interdys.org/ewebeditpro5/upload/ MSL2007finalR1.pdf

Made in the USA
Columbia, SC
28 June 2022